Coping With Redundancy

By

David A Ogden

Middle-aged and Redundant

Stuck In a Rut

Job Seeking

A story of how a 54 year old coped with being made redundant for the fourth time in ten years and a practical guide for the job seeker.

Copyright © David A. Ogden

All rights reserved

Published by David A. Ogden

First published in October 2004

ISBN 0-9548866-1-5

No part of this book may be reproduced in any Form without the permission of David A. Ogden

Foreword

This book has been written as a practical guide to help job seekers of any age find employment. The techniques described apply equally to any level of employment be it, manual work, semi-skilled, skilled, office administration, technical, management or executive search. This book will particularly benefit the middle age job seeker to cope with the trauma of redundancy and steps to find alternative employment.

The author of this book was made redundant four times at the age of 43, 44, 48 and 54. This book tells my story of how I coped with this tragedy, the trauma of being made redundant and a major disaster that have occurred in my working life. This book outlines my approach to coping with redundancy and the practical steps I took to find new employment. My approach proved very successful in that having been given two months advance warning of 'Threat of Redundancy' I secured a better position with a higher salary and improved benefits. The steps I took were basic and simple, following my approach will benefit people looking for new employment and the over forties who feel being made redundant as consigned them to the scrap heap.

Contents

	Page
Coping with trauma, tragedy and disaster	1
Out of the ashes	6
The end of an era the axe falls	10
Several new beginnings	16
The black spot strikes again	22
Redundancy disaster planning	24
Forward planning	25
Creating the CV	27
The power of using the internet	33
The un-advertised jobs market	35
Recruitment Agents	37
Job Centres and New Deal 50 Plus	38
Preparation for the interview	39
Appearance	41
Selling yourself at the interview	43
Outplacement counselling	45
Summary	47
Overview	48

Coping with Trauma, Tragedy and Disaster

"Its not what happens to you in life that's important its how you react to what happens, with thought you can turn any disaster into an advantage"

Source of quote unknown

In August 1972 I married my wife Kathleen, whilst on honeymoon in Newquay Cornwall I came across the above quotation in a newspaper. It struck me at the time as being a wedding present from God, I cut the clip out of the paper and have kept it in my wallet ever since. Like every one else on this planet I have suffered many traumas, tragedy, several mini disasters and one almighty disaster. On each of these occasions I have pulled the newspaper clip from my wallet and reflected on its meaning. I am very fortunate in that I have been gifted with a positive personality and I tend always to look for the positive aspects and things that I can do to influence and improve the situation. This book will give the reader an indication of some of the nasty things I've been faced with and how I turned them to my advantage.

30th September 1979, its 6.00am on a bright Sunday morning I'm stood in front of the television doing my ironing. I can't sleep my wife Kathleen is pregnant and has been in hospital for four weeks. Kathleen had 3 previous miscarriages, on this occasion she was ordered to take bed rest from the day it was confirmed she was pregnant again. Kathleen had spent 24 hours a day 7 days a week in bed until she reached 20 weeks; she was then allowed to get up for half a day. Kathleen was expecting twins, at 12 weeks we were informed that one of the twins was not developing and if it survived it would be severely handicapped. We were given the option of a termination; this was a very traumatic time for us. After a considerable amount of soul searching having had 3 previous miscarriages we decided to proceed with the pregnancy. At 28 weeks pregnant trauma struck again Kathleen's waters broke, contractions started and heart palpitations developed. Kathleen was rushed into hospital, to avoid the babies being born premature she was given drugs to stop the contractions and she talked of being in suspended animation.

I have never been a good sleeper and without Kathleen next to me in bed I suffered many restless nights and was often up before dawn. On this morning I had decided to get the ironing out of the way and then go off for a round of golf. At 6.15am a car speeds up the road and comes to a screeching halt in front of my window. I recognise the car as belonging to one of my work colleagues. He gets out of the car jumps over my garden wall and runs full pelt down the drive. As I open the door he greets me with the words "David, David the plants burned down come on lets go".

Are you sure I asked? yes my father rang me he heard it on the news, its bad there are 30 pumps attending. We got in the car and sped off at a hell of a speed, the plant was about six miles from my house, as we turned the corner and headed north we could see a huge black cloud. As we past Walkden, Manchester on the outskirts of Bolton about one and a half miles from the plant we realised just how bad the fire must have been. We past Lakefield which was a large lake, coming out of the lake were large water pipes, which had been laid to drain off water to fight the fire.

As we got to the plant there were hundreds of people stood watching, it was an awesome sight. We parked up the car and went into the canteen area where many employees had gathered, the fire was now out and the fire brigade were packing up and moving out with the exception of a number of senior firemen who were giving out safety warnings. We were informed the fire had started in the early evening and raged for most of the night. We slipped out through a side door and walked unseen over to a fire escape, which led to the roof, when we got to the top it was an incredible scene, the whole of the roof had collapsed into the factor shop floor. Multi million pound machines were still glowing cheery red there was carnage everywhere and the smell was awful. It was obvious over night 1,000 plus employees have lost their jobs. What was I going to tell my wife? I looked to the heavens and remember saying "what on earth I have done to deserve this on top of every thing else you've thrown at me over the last couple of months".

Working in teams organised by one of the managers we spent the rest of the day clearing up and trying to salvage what we could. We realised it was pretty much useless but just felt we had to do something, everyone was totally depressed and I remember seeing a very senior executive crying. He had been there most of the night and was obviously suffering from tiredness and had become very emotional. On seeing him I reflected on what was I going to tell my wife, with the stress she had suffered over the past months I really did not want to break this news to her. Fortunately when I got to the hospital later that evening she had seen it reported on the television news. It had been reported as the biggest fire ever in Europe since the war with an estimated cost around £50 million pounds. As you would imagine she was very distressed and worried how were we going to survive this disaster and how would I get another job with so many people out of work as a result of the fire. I tried to console her by saying there was always jobs for skilled and qualified engineers and that I had many strings to my bow having served both a mechanical apprenticeship followed by a technical apprenticeship and having recently qualified as a Work Study Organisation and Methods engineer so the world was my oyster, although I was feeling just as upset and disillusioned as she.

The next day being Monday I went into work as normal just to see what was happening. We had a very large canteen that was separate from the main building and was untouched by the fire, we also had a large assembly hall which was also unaffected by the fire. These turned out to be our saving grace, we were very fortunate to have forward thinking, talented, gifted and creative senior executives who had spent the previous day planning the way forward. These people were the Plant Manager who managed the site and the Operations Director who was based at our London European head office. The company was the Eaton Corporation a large American multi-national employing over 46,000 employees worldwide. At the time of the fire I was employed at Eaton Truck Components a division producing heavy-duty gear box transmissions. The truck components division had five plants in Europe and a similar number of plants in North America two of which produced the same product as we did in Manchester.

At 9.00am on that Monday morning we were addressed by the Plant Manager, he advised the meeting of an outline strategy that he was going to present with the Operations Director to the Eaton Board of Directors the next day at Eaton World Headquarters in Galesburg North America. The plan was simple, the group of two had recognised this was a golden opportunity to build a state of the art facility that would become the jewel in the crown of the European operation. The new plant would produce product at a significantly reduced cost base thus offering both comparative and competitive pricing with the new equipment contributing to higher levels of efficiency, productivity and quality product. It was recognised that the workforce at the Manchester plant had high skill levels, good employee relations and were already committed to the Eaton philosophy of excellence through people.

The strategy being put forward was that as the assembly hall was unaffected by the fire that components could be imported from North America and assembled on site utilising the existing workforce. Customer needs could be met initially by utilising under capacity at the American plants and working overtime. Plants at Basingstoke and St Nazaire in France produced similar products to that produced at the Manchester plant and also had spare capacity. Employees from the Manchester plant could be sent to work at both the Basingstoke and St Nazaire plants thus retaining the skilled workforce. There was also a new industrial estate close by with a vacant building that could be used as a machine shop. This then was the plan, which was sold and accepted, very quickly to the U.S. board and so plans were put in place to rebuild the Manchester plant.

I recognised this as my opportunity to take advantage of this disaster and offered my services to work on any areas the company felt I could best be used. I went out of my way to talk with as many senior people as possible to make it well known that I would take on any role. The company were exceptionally good to me, they were aware my wife was in hospital and fixed me up with a role that meant I could remain in Manchester until after my wife gave birth. On the 2 November 1979 Kathleen had problems again and a decision was taken by the doctors to deliver by caesarean section. At 7.35pm that Friday night my son Anthony was born premature, our second child was still born. The emotion of that night will never leave me I felt a volcano of stress erupt from my body within seconds of seeing my son to be replaced by overwhelming feelings of joy, calm and satisfaction at the end of what seemed like a lifetime of trauma and tragedy. This was our new beginning, the start of our life as a family, the futures bright the futures our son.

Out of the Ashes

A couple of months after the birth of Anthony I was seconded to work at the Basingstoke plant working as a Work Study engineer to establish methods and time standards for the work which was being transferred in from the Manchester plant. I considered myself to be very lucky to do this as I was home each weekend; many hundreds of my shop floor colleagues had a more difficult time. There were working a shift system where they rotated been Basingstoke and St Nazaire working three weeks at each site. So they were away from their families for a much longer period of time than I and suffered much more stress and inconvenience.

Back at the Manchester plant things were starting to take shape, the canteen had been converted into a large single story open plan office filled with lots of second hand equipment. Portakabins had been brought in to make up the short fall to occupy the remaining staff. The assembly hall was working as normal and the logistics staff were doing a superb job of co-ordinating material from America, Basingstoke and St Nazaire. The empty unit on the local industrial estate had been rented and filled with second hand and borrowed equipment and many manufacturing organisations around the UK had supported the effort and offered equipment on loan. Maintenance and Production engineers were working round the clock to commission this equipment and get it up and running. Output from the plant in terms of units per day was very quickly back up to normal although the cost of running the business were out the window and the site was obviously unprofitable although some of this was covered by insurance. I'm not sure of the detail or the timing but I am aware it was a very long time before the insurance on the building and equipment came through. It was the Corporation who fully supported the plant and the people and there were very few redundancies resultant from the fire.

The factory that had been destroyed in the fire was raised to the ground creating a green field site. A project team was put together to re-facilitate the site, this team worked on plant layout, workflows, capital equipment, capacity planning and manning levels. Twelve months into the programme I was invited to join this team and given responsibility for gear production working closely with the other engineers and capital equipment suppliers. I was responsible for process planning, workflows, purchase of capital equipment, installation and commissioning and training programmes. We were also one of the first organisations in the country to introduce Total Quality Management and gain certification of ISO9000 & BS5750. This was a very exciting time; every day brought new challenges, new learning, new problems to be resolved and tight dead lines to be achieved. The corporation had developed a wide-ranging business plan for the site, which included a substantial investment to introduce a large R&D organisation into the site to have responsibility for designing product aimed at Europe, Africa and Asia markets. These new products would be produced at the five European production plants, the future looked bright, prosperous and secure. I did not know it at the time but this decision was to be my path to significant career advancement.

In June 1982, 3 years after the fire the new plant was up and running and the Duke Of Edinburgh officially opened the plant. I remember seeing the Plant Manager who had masterminded the rebuilding of the site walking round with a huge grin on his face he was feeling very pleased and proud, and we were of him. We all had a lot to be grateful to him for, it was his vision, confidence in the workforce and management style that made this happen, the corporation recognised his ability and promoted him to Operations Director, he later went on to become Vice President of European Operations then went over to America to run the whole of the Truck Components Operation World-Wide. We all had a wonderful day and were given Wedgewood memorial plates embedded with the outline of the new plant. It was a day to remember with many events culminating in a large party held under a huge marquee. It was a very hot summers night the drink flowed and there was not a dry eye in the house as the music played and emotions overflowed. It was a night I will never forget and the memorial plate still has pride of place in my study along with a photograph of the new plant.

With the introduction of the European Product Engineering and R&D Business Unit came a flow of new product development. At first a trickle building up quickly to a fast flowing river. Eaton formed a joint development agreement with Iveco of Italy to design and develop a new medium duty range of gearbox transmissions. I was appointed to the position of New Product Introduction Manager with a brief to link Marketing, Product Management, Product Design Engineering with the five manufacturing plants. This was a huge and unexpected promotion for me it turned out to be a dream job, within months I had a very high profile and visibility on the European stage. Although I have held more senior positions since, this job gave me the most job satisfaction. I got to travel extensively throughout the world, to work closely with the five Plant Managers and their staff at Basingstoke, Manchester, Newton Aycliffe, St Nazaire and Pamplona. I was invited to join the Eaton/Iveco steering committee and spent a significant amount of time working in Italy. I was invited to join the Product Management Steering Group run by the Vice President European Operations where I represented the interests of the Plant Managers and occasionally deputised for the Operations Director and I got to develop a rapport with our supplier base.

I was operating in another world I could not ever imagine an opportunity like this would come along, here was I a working class lad an ex craft apprentice with only limited qualifications of a City & Guilds, ONC and Work Study qualifications working closely with highly qualified Vice Presidents, Directors, Plant and Commercial Managers, Product Management and Designers. My department reported to the European Purchasing Manager with a dotted line into the Operations Director. What I had not realised was that although I was poorly qualified by comparison my peer group had recognised from my previous successes that my street wise opportunistic style combined with my work study training had acquitted me with exceptional fundamental management skills and ability of planning, controlling, directing, coordinating, monitoring and prioritising work that enabled me to deliver in line with my commitments. The fact that I had the ability to prioritise work and was prepared to stand up and say I can't do that by that date but I will deliver by this date and did was recognised as a competent positive quality and strength.

Although on paper I reported into the Purchasing Manager, in operational terms I had significantly more daily dealings with the Operations Director and I was later promoted onto his staff. This Operations Director had a big influence on me, I observed him very closely, his management style, his way of doing things, how he motivated people, how he made things happen, in many ways we had a lot of similarities we were both results driven, worked long hours, recognised it was people who make the difference and made sure they got the recognition they deserved. But there the things we had in common ended, he was far more intelligent than I, more politically correct and had the patience to step back and work round obstacles whereas I was more direct had no patience and would steam roller over obstacles thus getting the job done more quickly but upsetting people along the way. My problem was over enthusiasm wanting results, wanting success, wanting to meet aims and objectives and deliver my commitments. You live and learn and as I've grown older, wiser, more experienced I've calmed down become more assertive less aggressive and more politically correct. The old saying is very true you can't put an old head on young shoulders, you learn by experience.

During my time working in new product introduction my wife gave birth to our second child. This was a text case pregnancy everything went extremely well. Neighbours took Anthony to play school enabling Kathleen to put her feet up and relatives called in during the day to help out. The pregnancy went full term and our daughter Katie was born 15 January 1994. I spent four years as New Product Introduction Manager, my work on the Eaton/Iveco joint development programme led to my next promotion. I was promoted to the position of Medium Duty Transmissions Operations Programme Implementation Manager, a real mouthful. In this role I would report directly to the Operations Director but work along side the Basingstoke Plant Manger with responsibility to introduce Medium Duty Transmissions. The role covered introducing a significant amount of new capital equipment, the introduction of a transmission assembly line, growth rate planning, TQM and continuous improvement teams, cost reduction team and operations management. It was my role to introduce this new product, set the plant up, run the operation, work with marketing to build up the business and then hand the product over to the Plant Manager as a going concern.

The End of an Era the Axe Falls

Having spent two years at Basingstoke introducing the medium duty transmission range the plant started to run into trouble. Basingstoke had become a Boom Town, being approximately 30 miles outside London on the M4 corridor it had become the place for commercial businesses to relocate to. The AA had already made its headquarters in the town and many insurance companies and financial institutions were opening up officers. Labour availability was scarce, unemployment was practically zero and companies were offering bonuses to employees who introduced new employees to their companies. Labour rates were increasing, land prices and rented office space and house prices escalated and rocketed to alarming levels and Eaton was unable to recruit new employees. On one occasion it took four months to recruit an electrian who stayed one month. Why work in a dingy factory when you could earn almost twice as much working in a newly opened office complex. Whilst many long serving employees remained loyal and stayed with the company many younger employees moved on. As they left the company it became increasingly more difficult to recruit replacements.

The final nail in the coffin for the Basingstoke plant was the landlords who owned the building. A few years before the contract on the building was due to be renewed they gave notice to Eaton that they would be raising the rent by a significant amount. They obviously wanted Eaton out in order to redevelop the land generating significantly higher financial returns than they would receive if they continued to lease the property to Eaton. This notification combined with the difficulty in recruiting new employees effectively signalled the closure of the Basingstoke plant. However well the management wanted to prevent rumours and speculation, I remember well the process of drip feeding information that went on, non the less when the announcement eventually came there was total devastation and disbelief amongst the workforce. We were all totally gutted, how could the corporation invest multi-millions of pounds in recent years only to pull out now the product was established. None the less the decision had been taken the plant would close with the loss of around 400 jobs.

The announcement was made that the Basingstoke plant would close and the medium duty transmission business would transfer to Eaton's plant at Newton Aycliffe, Co Durham where there was an adequate supply of skilled labour and operating overhead costs were more favourable. Other products were to be transferred to Manchester and St Nazaire. A simultaneous announcement was made at the Newton Aycliffe plant informing employees that they would lose the current axle business, which would go to the Pamplona plant in Spain. I was appointed to the position of Project Manager with responsibility to manage the transition of business out of the Basingstoke plant and into Aycliffe, Manchester and St Nazaire. I had already started work on this plan well in advance of the announcement and was able to quickly move out the work and consolidate business into the Manchester and St Nazaire plants. The transfer of work into Newton Aycliffe was more complex, large machining centres had to be moved along with banks of cnc machines, hobbing, shaping, shaving gear cutting machines, grinding machines, broaching machines and a whole host of other specialised equipment.

Large banks of work in progress components had to be built up before equipment could be transferred. Employees from the Aycliffe plant had to come to Basingstoke and spend many weeks and some cases months training to learn new jobs, equipment and machines. This was a significant strain on employees from both plants having to deal with the stress of forming a close working relationship with a person who's job you are going to take. All credit to the folks at Basingstoke they held there heads high acted in a highly professional manner and there was not one instance of sabotage or falling out with the folks from Newton Aycliffe. The same applied to the folks from Newton Aycliffe. Many were very reluctant to make the journey down to Basingstoke they felt they were unable to work with and form relationships with people who's jobs they were taking. After all they were brothers in the same engineering union they encountered many mixed and emotional feelings. Many Newton Aycliffe employees needed counselling before they would go, many others declined to go at the last minute. These are traumas and emotions that many UK employees have gone through since the mass exit began in 1985. As more and more businesses close down plants, consolidate and transfer business, these are emotions and feelings that once we have tasted them never go away and remain always at the back of our minds.

Having put the relocation plan together and issued the programme to Basingstoke and Newton Aycliffe management teams I transferred to the Newton Aycliffe plant and took on the role of Production Control and Planning Manager. The Newton Aycliffe plant had also appointed a Project Manager to oversee the exit of the axle business and entry of the transmission business. Over the course of the next twelve months I worked very closely with this Project Manager and also the Manufacturing Manager at Basingstoke. It was us three who made things happen. My outline plan was the catalyst for the transition and was refined as we went along.

Approximately twelve months into the plan tragedy struck again, the recession had started bite, orders were falling away. The Manchester plant the jewel in the crown of the European operation was hit as a result of the down turn in American markets. U.S. plants were running under capacity and work was being pulled back from the Manchester operation. Corporate bean counters made their presence felt, cost had to be taken out of the European operation and the axe fell on the Newton Aycliffe Plant. We were all totally devastated, this was unexpected, unforeseen, unplanned it couldn't possibly be happening. Wrong it was and it did.

The corporate short-term plan was simple and effective; the transfer of product out of Basingstoke and into Newton Aycliffe would stop immediately. Instead the product would transfer into the Manchester plant to take up the spare capacity vacated by product taken back to America. All manufacturing would cease at Newton Aycliffe and transfer into Manchester with the exception of assembly, large machining centres and synchronisers, which required specialist knowledge. The work force would reduce from 500 plus down to 100 and become a satellite operation reporting into the Manchester Plant Manager. All managers but one would become redundant and that would be at the level of a Manufacturing Manager rather than the traditional site Plant Manager. The longer-term plan was to buy a plant in

Poland and transfer all manufacturing and assembly into this facility generating substantial savings in operating costs. So then David get out of this one, I couldn't. Events had eventually caught up with me, aged 43 and having spent 26 years of my working life with the same company and fully expecting to be with them until my retirement I find I am redundant and out of a job.

What's more I'm in a strange land. I've brought my wife and family to this place called Newton Aycliffe, Co Durham. We have no family or friends in this area and no one to turn to for support. We are outsiders in an extremely hostile environment, we have lived in the area a little over twelve months I've taken on a huge mortgage to buy a bigger house than we really need to enable friends and family to come and visit us. I bought my house at the top end of the market and the value had tumbled in recent months, I am now sitting on negative equity, for want of other more suitable words, we as a family are well and truly in the **SHIT.**

Well that's the negative aspects out of the way or is it? and have you every noticed they always tell you this on a Friday giving you the weekend free to get over the disappointment and expecting you back in on Monday refreshed and raring to go. **Bollocks,** that's not the way it works, for most people depression sets in, you ask yourself questions why me? why have they chosen me? I'm conscientious, I work hard, I have a good attendance record, I have excellent work appraisals and I get on well with everyone, they must have got this wrong. In a situation like I was in these types of questions were irrelevant as almost everyone was being made redundant but in a work situation where only a small percentage of people are targeted for redundancy they are very valid questions. In these instances you need to focus on the positive and prepare your case for defence do not lie back and let it happen make the HR department and your manager work hard to prove you have not been unfairly chosen. There are procedures and processes to be followed, European legislation is such that it is now longer a tap on the shoulder, your it and out the door you go, stand and fight your corner and if your not happy go to tribunal. At worst you will lose your case but many win extra compensation and others settle out of court.

In my case we had a miserable Friday night we were all depressed, worried, concerned for the future, concerned about finances, we had all read in the newspapers and seen on the television the over forties can't get jobs, the end of the world had come. That is until I went to my wallet and read that newspaper clip, the words "you can turn any disaster to an advantage" to an advantage, to an advantage, to an advantage, got it!

Yes I've got it, my positive side took over again I drafted out the advantages of being made redundant.

1. A large chunk of money that would meet all my outgoings for a year.

2. This was the kick in the backside I needed to go out and Advance my career.

3. We can go and have a dam good well-deserved holiday.

4. So I was over 40 what of it? What about all the wide ranging experience I have built up, someone out there must value it.

5. So I'm away from family and friends what does that matter sure they would be a shoulder to cry on and give me some sympathy but they can't contribute to finding me a new job.

6. The Northeast is a big place with good infrastructure and easy of access to Newcastle, Sunderland, Middlesbrough, Darlington and Bishop Auckland. A multitude of local daily newspapers and job centres to compliment the Telegraph and Times.

7. I can use this opportunity to search for a new job back in Manchester.

8. I've got several months breathing space to secure a new position so there is no point in panicking.

So there you have it there were many advantages to being made redundant and we could well end up being substantially financially better off we should be cheering instead of weeping. I put a plan together to seek new employment, which I will outline in a later chapter. I secured a new position within a month left Eaton and moved into a more senior better-paid position with a higher quality car and better benefits.

Several New Beginnings

I left the Eaton Corporation in April 1992 and walked straight into a job with Cascade (UK) Ltd. I took on the role of Manufacturing Manager with responsibility for production, tool room, maintenance, quality and production engineering. Cascade were a small American Corporation employing around 5,000 in the U.S and Europe. They had one plant in the U.K. and three in the Netherlands centred in Amsterdam. My association with Cascade was not a long one nor was it particularly a happy one. The Managing Director and I had different styles and expectations. For all we clashed I actually liked the guy he was good company and we had similar personalities just different styles and ten months into the job I got the bullet along with a substantial compensation package. Fortunately I had foreseen this coming and I had already commenced the process of seeking alternative employment although this time I was targeting the Northwest.

I was unemployed for only three weeks; I used this time to further develop and build on my methods of seeking a new position and learnt the technique of networking. I also relaxed by playing a lot of golf and got my garden ship shape. I next moved to Combine Power Systems Ltd as Plant Manager again a move up the ladder and again more money. I was very successful at Combined Power Systems I was given a free hand and had total autonomy to run the organisation how I liked. CPS was a new company that had only been in business about 4 years, the Chief Executive, founder and main shareholder was an amazing man. He had previously made his millions from running a chain of car showrooms. One day he read an article on the benefits of utilising combined heat and power. He had the vision and creativity to see the possibilities of such a system sold off his car business went back to university to do a degree in thermal dynamics. Then working with Manchester University built his first Combined Heat and Power Generator. Four years on when I joined the company they were producing 20 units a month had just announced a £1.5 million pound profit and had started to lay the foundations of a new plant on a green field site.

For a work-study man an ex production engineer and coming from the automotive industry joining CPS was like receiving manner from heaven. The opportunities for implementing improvements, increasing output, efficiency, productivity and driving costs down were endless. On top of this I was given a new factory with a blank sheet of paper and almost an open chequebook to equip it. Working closely with the lads on the shop floor they bought into my ideas to introduce team based work systems and automotive style production flow line approach to building the units. I got several of the lads involved in designing workstations and working with suppliers to develop a process flow that would almost treble our production capacity and more than doubled our productivity. In doing this we were successful in removing all layers of supervision and the team leaders ran the business. We developed a good family type atmosphere, we had an excellent working environment, good safe working conditions, I was able to negotiate a self financing 10% pay rise and change in hours of work to enable the lads to finish work at lunch time on Friday. In a short space of time we had developed into a friendly effective working unit, we all had nicknames the lads affectionately referred to me as 'Hilda' for obvious reasons of my sir name and us being within a few miles of Granada Television Studios.

My reward for generating this level of improvement and success was to be promoted to Operations Manager and take on other areas of the business. My confidence was shy high this was a million miles away from my experience at Cascade. I fully expected to be with Combine Power Systems until my retirement, I was doing a job that I enjoyed and working with a great bunch of lads, and the Chief Executive gave me a completely free hand, life was wonderful. We have all heard the saying all good things come to an end and so it was to be at CPS. Black clouds were gathering on the horizon the end was near. The company had been taken over by three electrical utility providers, London Electric, Northern Electric and NORWEB. Although I was a senior executive manager I was not on the board and therefore not privy to privileged confidential information I was aware the company was experiencing some commercial difficulty and sales were dropping off but it came totally out of the blue when we were notified production operations, design and installation were to be closed down and phased out, the company would in future only focus on the service side of the business we were all dumbstruck.

And so it was redundancy had struck again now aged 48 I was once again heading towards the dole queue. Once again I got my newspaper clip out and focused on those words *"Its not what happens to you in life that's important its how you react to what happens, with thought you can turn any disaster into an advantage"*. I had not given any thought whatsoever over the course of the last three years to the possibility of being made redundant again. It just wasn't a consideration we had a new plant, new equipment and a superb technically advanced product, which had just won the Queens Award for the Environment. How on earth could production be wound up, it was just unbelievable a dream I was going to wake up soon. Well I didn't wake up it was true the company had run into some financial problems and we would soon close. Again we were lucky that we had some time before the plant closed to complete our work in progress and working in Manchester there was a large employer base advertising jobs.

I was lucky in that I had three avenues of opportunity; fortunately due to depressed market conditions I had been unable to sell my house in Co Durham. I had been living in Manchester with two of my elderly ants Flo & Mary who lived very close to where I was working. This worked very well as they loved me to bits and spoilt me something shocking and I was around to do all those little jobs that came up. And of course they fed back to Kathleen all the info on what I was getting up to. Living with my aunts gave me the opportunity of looking for work in three geographic regions and using my previously developed job seeking technique had many thousands of companies to target in the Northwest, Northeast and West Yorkshire. I also needed to consider my children this time my son Anthony would soon be starting his GCSE years so I had his education needs to consider and I also wanted to be with him to help him through it. After writing 800 hundred plus letters, attending dozens of interviews and travelling thousands of miles up and down the motorway two-job offers arrived during the same week. One a General Manager position in Knutsford, Cheshire the other a much lesser job of Product Leader based in Darlington, Co Durham about 10 miles from where I lived.

We had a very difficult job to decide what should I do, should I take the General Manager role which was £5k more than I was earning at CPS or take the Product Leader role which was £15k less and no car but on the door step in Darlington. After deliberating for days the choice became very clear, family first career second my son was young he needed to get his GCSE's and me working 200 miles down the road was of no use, I needed to be there to support, help and give him guidance and encouragement.

I chose to accept the job of Product Leader with Cummins Engine Company Ltd. One of the secondary reasons for me accepting the job with Cummins was the fact that this organisation was a large American Corporation. I considered that because I had worked previously for a bigger American Corporation at an executive level that it would only be a matter of time before my ability and skills were recognised and promotion would be imminent. How wrong I was, I did not allow for the regional differences in culture or the fact Cummins had been founded on a Societal Product Concept. One of the founders of Cummins had religious beliefs, people really do matter to Cummins who took a much softer approach to running the business than the much harder results driven make it happen style I was use to with the Eaton Corporation.

Cummins Engine Company Inc, was founded in 1919 by Clessie J. Cummins, a self taught mechanical inventor who was intrigued by the potential of Rudolf Diesel's thermally efficient theory. The local banker called William Clanton Irwin provided backing for the firm. The Irwin family held very religious beliefs; this resulted in many charitable donations, community projects and works schemes. This combination led to the growth and expansion of the business and the philosophy of prosperity for all and the development of a company that could be constructed as following a Societal Product Concept.

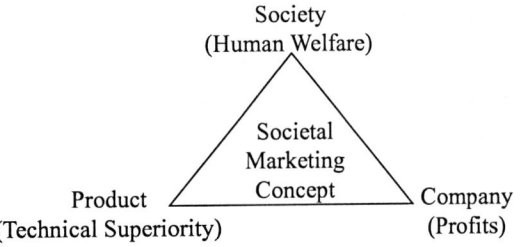

Figure 1: Societal Product Concept

And so it was I had to adjust and learn a new culture, develop a new management style to fit with my new environment. This did not come easy to me it took me many years to adjust, with Eaton I had been indoctrinated into a highly dynamic way of doing things quickly and effectively, if a direct report failed to deliver then he/she would get a rocket up there backside. With Cummins it was a case of putting your arm round their shoulder and asking, What went wrong? What can I do to help you? Do you need any addition training and development? The one thing that really irritated me at Cummins was the lack of meeting discipline, people didn't turn up, arrived late, were ill prepared or had not done the work. At Eaton these people would have been given an absolute roasting they would have been up the road in no time, this level of underperformance would not be tolerated.

In my role as Product Leader I was responsible for customer driven engineering change and new product introduction. I co-ordinated all aspects of the process from quotation through the various phases of design and release processing, materials management, manufacturing engineering, quality, customer service, shop operations through to production readiness. When I commenced this role I was amazed at how inefficient and ineffective this process was, for a large corporation I expected this would have been a well-organised and tightly controlled process. There was little information available on through put times only one performance measure and the process was pretty much a black hole. Product Change Requests (PCR's) were submitted and at some point in time in the future they would emerge as a new option on a customer shop order. The company had been receiving many customer complaints about the under performance of the process and lack of information on status and introduction dates which led to my appointment.

For me this job was an absolute doddle (easy peasy for the folks who do not understand Manchester speak) having previously run a new product introduction function I new exactly what to do to turn this process into a 'Best Practice'. These issues around the process were related to lack of management of the process, lack of performance measures and an ineffective organisational allocation or resource. The process was not adequately controlled and the PCR team that was in place at the time had many other tasks to look after which prevented them for working on PCR's. Based on available data average quotation times were 35 days and average introduction times were 311 days, far to excessive in today's cutthroat competitive world.

I won't go into detail of what we did or how we did other than to say I was instrumental in setting up three cross-functional teams:

Management team	Focus on organisational development and business processes.
PCR team	Focus on the process and work elements of what was done, how it was done, elimination of waste and ineffective elements of work etc.
	Introduction of project management techniques.
Systems team	Introduction of an electronic process and database giving visibility of status and performance measures.

Introduction times fell at a rapid rate and during the period 1999- 2001 we achieved an average time of 5 days for quotations and 62 days for introduction a very substantial improvement down from 311 days where we started.

The Black Spot Strikes Again

2000 and 2001 and had not been good years for Cummins, the engine business is very much a cyclic product. I was use to this with Eaton as transmissions fell into the same category. Truck sales are very much a barometer of economies. When recession rears its head road transport and sales of trucks are very noticeably affected. Slowing sales in the high street impact on the transportation of goods, which in turn affects the numbers of trucks, sold. Cummins Darlington plant suffered several bouts of redundancy during 2000 and 2001 and in September 2001 we were advised that more redundancies were on the way and that negotiations with the unions had commenced.

10.30am Friday 12th November 2001, (yes Friday again) I received a phone call from the HR department asking me to pop down and see them. I make my way to personnel where I am directed into a conference room there I am greeted by my Line Manager and HR Manager and invited to sit down. Of course I know what's coming, I'm informed, *"David I'm very sorry to inform you that your role is transferring to our U.S. process and you are being issued with Threat Of Redundancy"*. Imagine how I am feeling I'm within months of my 54th birthday, I've had five annual appraisals in a row all commending me as having performed outstandingly well. I've been responsible for substantially improving the PCR process to the best process any where in the corporation and I'm now being told I'm no longer required, I was gutted absolutely gutted.

I was then informed *"as of today you are not redundant and there may be some opportunity for you to move into another role in the event some volunteers come forward to take early retirement"*. Consoling words buts words that went right over my head as far as I was concerned I was redundant and I probably had until year-end to find a new position. **This time I was prepared, very well prepared with military precision.** At the first sign of redundancy four years earlier I started work on my Disaster Planning. I had foreseen this day coming and there was no way I was going to let redundancy in my fifties get me down. I was on the page of using this disaster to my advantage and to be my stepping-stone to a more senior position. Both Anthony and Katie had passed their GCSE's, Anthony had just finished university and Katie was only months away from completing her Diploma course at college so family issues were no longer a problem. I got home that Friday night went to my computer and commenced implementing my plan, details of which are contained in the next chapter.

November and December are traditionally show months in recruitment with not many jobs advertised in the papers so it was important to get into the un-advertised jobs market by using agents and mail shots. My plan covers how I went about this task. Days before I was due to be made redundant I was offered an alternative position, which I accepted, this position however turned out to be very short lived. I started my new job on the 2nd January 2002 as a Customer Services Rep. On Tuesday 8th of January 2002 we were asked to attend a video conference call with the U.S. On that call the department I had just moved into were informed that a decision to outsource Customer Service had been taken a contract had been signed and the external vendor would take over the business from the 1st March 02. Doom and gloom around the room, 14th January 02, I was again issued with notification of Threat Of Redundancy.

Having set my job-seeking plan into action a couple of months earlier invitations to attend interview were now starting to arrive. On top of this I continued to search job advertisements in the papers, and Internet sites and continued with my attack on the un-advertised sector by sending out mail shots to targeted organisations. Cummins were exceptionally supportive I was allowed many days off work on authorised absence to travel up and down the country to attend interviews. Several opportunities also arose at Cummins most of which were lesser-paid jobs than that I was currently doing including one senior manager role as an SQI Quality Manager. A job I had not done before on a full time basis but I did have some experience of SQI gained during my time as New Product Introduction Manager some fourteen years earlier. I applied for this job, although I was a rank outsider for this position my philosophy is *'you've got to be in it to win it'* and *'if you don't have a go you'll never know'*. Week commencing 18th February 02 two job offers come in, week commencing 25th February 02 I get offered the SQI Managers job with Cummins.

Redundancy Disaster Planning

Steps:

1   Forward Planning.

2   Creating the CV.

3   The power of using the Internet.

4   The un-advertised jobs market.

5   Recruitment agents.

6   Jobcentres

7   Preparation for the interview

8   Appearance

9   Selling your self at the interview.

10 Outplacement counselling.

Forward Planning

My forward planning began four years earlier; I had already developed my strategy and redundancy disaster plan. All I needed to do now was refine the plan and add to it to take account of the advancements in information technology and the power of the Internet.

In today's rapidly shrinking and competitive world we employees have to recognise that the word 'competition' doesn't just apply to companies competing against one another it applies equally to us ordinary folks in the workplace. There is rarely a week goes by without we see something on the television news about organisations downsizing, consolidating or in the case manufacturing companies focusing on introducing learner, meaner manufacturing processes. We hear about Total Quality Management, Kiazen, Six Sigma, Continuous Improvement Teams, Quality Circles and Speed Workshops all techniques aimed at taking cost out of the product and ultimately leading to head count reduction. These initiatives are all designed to lower operating costs and drive more profit into the bottom line thus making the organisation more financial secure and better placed to survive. The bottom line is, however painful these actions are, they are necessary for the benefit of the organisation to survive and to secure the future for those employees lucky enough to remain with the organisation.

We employees therefore have to recognise that we must become more competitive in the workplace. We must meet our targets, achieve our performance measures, be positive, focused, join improvement teams, work with the management and each other to improve processes and strive for excellence in all that we do. More than this we must plan our self-development. In my case I recognised I had immense competition, all around me the organisation was packed full of highly qualified degree level people. You would expect this in a technical function, but in Cummins it was everywhere, the girls in Customer Service had HND's and degrees, some were studying MBA's, the folks in Marketing had degrees and MBA's . Although I was a very experienced manager I could not rely on my past record I had to get an MBA and aged 51 I went back to school or should I say university on the MBA programme. I did this on afternoon release and evening classes supported by Cummins. I also went to Sight and Sound academy of typing and learnt to type.

My forward plan:

- Develop my redundancy disaster plan.

- Get better Qualifications, gain an MBA.

    Learn to type, this would enable me to have better keyboard skills in the workplace and speed up the typing of my university assignments. I would also learn layout and Presentation.

- Attend as many as possible of the in house training courses learn the new techniques and volunteer to work on teams to apply them.

- Create a higher quality CV, do this by applying for jobs through agents then at the end of the interview question them on the layout and presentation of my CV determine its strengths and weaknesses. How can the CV be improved?

- Learn how to tap into the un-advertised jobs market.

- Work hard in the workplace; always be positive and willing to take on anything that I am asked to do. Make sure targets are achieved and make sure the annual appraisal gains high Ratings.

- Read books on interview technique and preparation.

- Identify high quality headhunters and recruitment agencies.

- Identify Internet recruitment web sites.

- Read up on networking.

Creating the CV

There are many books available on creating the perfect CV, I would advise readers to go to the library and read through these books to obtain a consensus of opinion on the perfect format. Remember your CV is a marketing tool that highlights your abilities and capabilities; you must present yourself in the best possible light as it will secure you interviews. I offer here my version I know it works because I got invited to lots of interviews. I also developed it through discussions with many agents so I know my format is in line with what they appear to be looking for. Having said that there are of course now many tens of thousands of recruitment agents out there so there are equally many thousands of different opinions on what a good CV looks like.

I have designed my CV to focus on the basics and to present outline facts giving the reader a concise snapshot of my career history and achievements. With reference to career history I have focused on five category headings:

Current Employer.
Company Profile.
Job Title.
Responsibilities.
Key Achievements.

Be creative but be honest, often your previous roles may match or be similar to the position advertised but the tile is different, you therefore may need to flex you CV to target it to fit the outline of the candidate profile.

Page 28 presents an example CV.

John Smith MBA FMS

ADDRESS

36 Any Road, Any Town, Any County, A1 AA1

Telephone: 1000 100000

E-mail: johnsmith@talent100.com

EDUCATION	University of Durham
	Manchester Polytechnic
	Stretford Technical College
QUALIFICATIONS	Degree of Masters of Business Administration
	Diploma Business Administration
	Diploma Management Services
	ONC Mechanical Engineering
	City & Guilds Mechanical Engineering
AGE	Born 30 March 1948
MARITAL STATUS	Married with 2 children
INTERESTS	Aerobics, Golf, Gym & Writing

Personal Profile

Talented Manager with extensive management experience gained in a manufacturing environment within large and small multi-national corporations. 30 years experience of producing quality engineered products within the European automotive industry. An accomplished man manager and inspirational team leader with outstanding communication skills, a change agent with a proven track record.

Proven ability to create growth in revenue and profits driving costs down through structured cost-effective strategic corporate planning and utilising TQM, Kiazen and continuous improvement and cost reduction programmes.

Project managed two green field start-ups and four major new products launches.

MBA Profile

MBA:	Degree of Masters of Business Administration.
Sponsor:	Aerospace PLC.
Dissertation:	An evaluation of customer driven new product introduction at Aerospace PLC.

Employment Record

Current Employer: Entronic Engines PLC   Oct 95-Present

Company Profile: Largest independent manufacturer of diesel engines employing in excess of 26,000 employees worldwide. Market segments include automotive, Industrial, rail, marine, filtration and turbo charger applications.

Job Title: Programme Timing Manager

Responsibilities: Commercial and technical customer focused role managing new product introduction and new business opportunities from quotation through: design, development, implementation and product launch. Also manage continuous improvement teams.

Key Achievements: Launch of Xray mid range engine on time in budget.

Quotations reduced from average 55 days to 5 days.

Introduction lead-time on ancillary interface products reduced from an average 311 days to 62 days.

Plant benched marked World-Class Best In Class resultant from my leadership.

Previous Employers: Power Generators Limited   Apr 93-Sep 95

Company Profile: Young rapidly expanding company competing in the combined heat and power generation market sector. CHP generators being installed in hotels, blocks of Flats, leisure centres, army & air force barracks, government buildings & Buckingham Place.

Job Title:	General Manager Operations
Responsibilities:	P&L for 3 Business Units Manufacturing Plant Installation Design & Contracting National Service Organisation £7 million turnover, 185 staff
Key Achievements:	Commenced as Plant Manager promoted to General Manager. Profitability increased by £1.2 million over 2.5 years. 60% increase in output by assembly layout redesign. $4 million green field site development + ISO9000 accreditation. Introduction of TQM & Continuous improvement teams. Introduction of Team Based Work System. Elimination of shop floor management and supervision.
Previous Employers:	Kansus (UK) Limited May 92-Apr 93
Company Profile:	Small American corporation, market sector truck components. Worldwide workforce of 5,000, main products hydraulic cylinders.
Job Title:	General Manager
Responsibilities:	P&L and site responsibility for design, marketing, production, assembly, finance, purchasing, production control, quality, production engineering. maintenance and tool room, workforce operating on a 2 and 3 shift system. Organise, direct and co-ordinate manufacturing resources in line with customer requirements. £9 million turnover, 185 staff.
Key Achievements:	Turnover increased by £700,000. Profitability increased by £160,000 Revised factory layout, introduction of cellular production. ISO 9000 accreditation. Introduction of TQM and continuous improvement teams.
Previous Employers:	Pluto Corporation Sep 63-Apr 92

Company Profile:	Large American corporation, diversified product range market sectors include: Space programme, electronic controls and truck components. 46,000 employees, blue chip Fortune 300 company.	
Location:	Pluto Components York	Jun 90-Apr 92
Job Title:	General Manager	
Responsibilities:	P&L and site responsibility, annual output 25,000 gearbox transmissions, 5,000 axels. £50+ million turnover, high volume production utilising CAD/CAM, CIM, AIMS linked to cnc machining facilities incorporating cellular, flow line and batch production methods. Unionised workforce 550 staff.	
Key Achievements:	Increased profitability resultant from TQM continuous improvement activity and the introduction of Kiazen, Kanban and Poke Yoke techniques.	
	Head count reduction from organisational restructuring.	
	£2 million inventory reduction, increase in material turns from 9 to 14.	
	Successful transfer of business from Basingstoke Plant.	
Location:	Pluto Components Basingstoke	Jun 87-Jun 90
Job Title:	General Manager	
Responsibilities:	P&L and site responsibility, annual output 15,000 gearbox transmissions, assortment of ancillary products and spare parts. £30 million turnover high volume production utilising CAD/CAM, CIM, AIMS linked to cnc machining facilities incorporating cellular, flow line and batch production methods. Unionised workforce 350 staff.	
Key Achievements:	Commenced as Operations Manager promoted to General Manager.	
	New Product launch of Medium Duty Transmissions.	
	$20 million capital equipment installation.	

Revised plant layout, productivity and efficiency gains.

Increased turnover and profitability.

Introduction of TQM and continuous improvement teams.

ISO 9000 accreditation

Location:	Pluto Components Manchester	Sep 63-Jun 87

Various Positions:	New Product Introduction Manager Europe (4 years)
Controlled major new product launches at 5 European plants.
Pioneered the introduction of SQA with the supply base.
Project Manager. (1of 4) (3 years)

$45 million Green field site development responsibility for gear manufacture, factory layout, capital equipment and to pioneer the introduction of TQM and ISO 9000 accreditation.

Production Engineer Gear Manufacture. (3 years)
Work Study Organisation & Methods Engineer (4years)
Technical Apprentice. (4 years)
Mechanical Apprentice. (6years)

The Power of Using the Internet

The Internet is a very powerful and simple tool for the job seeker to use and exceptionally user friendly to the beginner. I'm not a computer nerd, I'm not an advance user, I'm not even at intermediate level but I have learnt the basics and would consider myself to be just about computer literate. I'm familiar with Word, Excel, and Project Management. You do not however need any of this to use the Internet; all you need is a basic cheap computer set up to access the Internet. Then you simply type in the addresses of a few search engines like www.hotbot.com, www.google.com, www.jeeves.com and Bob's your uncle your on line. Selecting any or all one after the other you simple type in "UK Jobs" or "UK recruitment agencies" or narrow it down to "Manchester recruitment agencies" click on search and the computer will bring up a list of websites for you to visit.

You can then register on line with these agencies, enter your CV and search through the range of vacancies currently listed as available. If a vacancy takes your fancy you click the button to apply on line and your application is automatically submitted. Once you have registered many of these web sites will automatically forward you Email alerts notifying you of new jobs that have just become available. Two of my favourite websites are:

www.gojobsite.co.uk

This is a brilliant website used by the recruitment industry, once you are registered you can authorise the site to make your CV visible to recruitment agents. The site will send out regular Email alerts, in my case I got them almost daily notifying me of jobs that had just been registered. You can then click on the jobs you are interested in and it will bring up a job description, if you are interested you simply click on the apply button. In addition recruiters will view your CV on line and contact you by phone or Email if you are of interest to them. The site also gives details of how many times your CV has been viewed by recruiters. My CV had over 500 hits in three weeks, incredible.

www.jimfinder.co.uk

This is a similar site to gojobsite except it is solely for jobs in manufacturing. Again you get regular Email alerts and you can apply for the jobs on line.

Another source of finding website addresses is to look in the national newspapers like the Daily Telegraph or the Sunday Times. Most of the jobs advertised carry website addresses so you can very quickly build up a very large databank of recruitment agents. This gives the jobseeker significant opportunities to surf the web in a concerted effort to find new employment.

I had many calls from recruitment agents and several interviews as a direct result of registering my CV and applying for jobs on line.

A few other useful websites to get you started.

www.odgers.com

www.normanbroadbent.com

www.bberecruitment.co.uk

www.jobs.telegraph.co.uk

The un-advertised Jobs Market.

To attack this market will cost you money, time and effort but the reward of securing a new position justifies the means. If you want a job you have to be prepared to explore every avenue of opportunity. The un-advertised jobs market covers organisations that are thinking about advertising a vacancy, or contacting an agent or may not yet have a vacancy at the present but will have one in the not to distant future. The technique to attack this market is very simple, you mass mail shot every organisation in a geographical area either en-mass or by business sector, i.e., Engineering, Banking, Insurance, Retail etc. This is very simple to do, you start off by targeting a specific area/areas, in my case this was:

Newcastle, Sunderland, Middlesborough, Darlington, Bishop Auckland, Leeds, Bolton, Blackburn, Salford, Manchester, Leyland, Preston and Warrington. All within a one-hour drive of my home in Durham or my aunties in Manchester, actually the majority of these were within a thirty-minute drive. Next you look up the Chamber of Commerce or the local Town Hall make a phone call and find out where to obtain the local business directory. This will list all the businesses in the area by product category and detail address and telephone numbers. You then target the business segment you are interested in write out your speculative letter of application and start your mail shot.

Don't expect a flood of replies it won't happen you will be lucky to get 5% of companies replying and most of them will not have any vacancies. Don't despair sooner or later you letter will hit the right desk or a company will get back to you at a later date with an invitation to interview. Remember this is part of a strategic plan utilising a range of tactical options aimed at getting your bum on that interview seat. The more tactical options you use the sooner your objective will be achieved.

The next technique to use is networking. You simply contact people you know, friends, ex workmates, managers, companies, friends of friends, just about any one you come into contact with. You put the word out you are looking for a job, you get them to enquiry at their place of work, you phone up potential leads and explore every avenue of opportunity.

Recruitment Agents

Having created you CV immediately register with all your regional recruitment agencies. You can get their addresses from Yellow pages, or www.yellowpages.com and local newspapers. Your main post office will have the yellow pages for other towns and cities in your vicinity. For example if you live in Manchester the main post office would have the yellow pages for Bolton, Blackburn, Preston, Warrington, Wigan etc. You can also use a search engine on the Internet to find and identify local, regional, national and specialist agencies such as financial and accounting, education, scientific, manufacturing, manual, office administration etc.

Register with as many agents as possible, remember though that recruitment agents are there to serve their clients needs not the candidates. Having registered with the agent your details will be entered onto their database this is another link into the un-advertised jobs sector. If you are out of work or under threat of redundancy at the time of registration you should consider informing the agent that you will consider part time, temporary, interim and permanent positions.

When applying for positions in response to advertisements placed by agents it is important to tailor your letter of application to meet the candidate profile. Look for the key words in the job advertisement relating to skills, ability and experience. Your letter of application should be sharp, brief, concise and focused on identifying your suitability for the position. As with creating your CV this is something you need to practice and develop in advance. Do as I did and develop your letter writing technique as part of your forward planning, when you attend interviews get feed back on your letter of application as well as your CV. Find out what were the key points that resulted in you being short listed.

I had around twenty standard letters on file that I flexed in relation to the role and the candidate profile these were all streamlined and improved following consultation with agents to be, brief, bright and focused.

Job Centres

Job centres have been amazingly transformed over the course of the last few years. On the last occasion I visited a job centre back in 1995 I found them to be very unfriendly places. I found the staff to be typical stereotype civil servants they were very stern faced and neither friendly nor particularly helpful. Today they have been refurbished and transformed into highly efficient centres utilising state of the art information technology. From a terminal in your local job centre you now have the opportunity to search the data bank of job vacancies at a local, regional or national level. At the job centres close to where I live I found the staff to be of the highest calibre they were extremely friendly and very helpful. On my first visit I asked one of the staff to give me some guidance on using the newly installed terminals. He spent 30 minutes training me to use the equipment and made sure I was fully conversant before he left me. He also explained that many of the front line staff had been recruited from the long term unemployed so you can be sure of receiving a sympathetic ear.

One tip, take a flask and sandwiches. The job centres are now quite plush and comfortable and you could be in there for many hours searching out that new job. You will also find a range of leaflets and booklets giving advise and guidance to help you plan your strategy.

New Deal 50 Plus

This scheme has been set up to help the over 50's who have been out of work for over six months. New Deal 50 Plus is helping unemployed people by bringing together different organisations in local partnerships to create opportunities of work and training. Many people over 50 find it difficult to find a worthwhile job that pays a decent wage. The scheme offers job seekers a wide range of practical help including a Personal Advisor. They will give help with preparing your CV, suggest training courses, support to develop your self-confidence and help you to consider available opportunities. This scheme also enables the job seeker to claim Employment Credit and Training Grant. Apply through your local Jobcentre.

Preparation for the Interview

- Obtain a map and directions by contacting the company receptionist.

- Research the company's background and product range.

   a) Look on the company website, you can get this address from the receptionist.

   b) If the company is PLC contact the Times newspaper ask them to send out a copy of the Annual Report. This is a free service.

   c) If no website and not a PLC ring the sales and marketing department say you are a student undertaking a project and could they send you out some literature on the companies products.

- Anticipate possible questions.

   Questions relating to career background.

   Questions relating to your covering letter and CV.

   Questions relating to management style.

   Questions relating to the product range.

   Questions relating to technical aspects or organisational issues.

   What skills do you bring relative to the job that will benefit the organisation.

   What makes you the most suitable candidate for the position.

Examples of questions I've been asked.

Why do you want to join this organisation?

What range of competencies do you have?

Describe your management style?

What type of budgeting techniques are you familiar with?

What are your strengths and weaknesses?

How do you deal with under performing people?

If you get the job what is the first thing you would do?

What steps would you take to motive your team?

In 3 words describe the role of a manager?

What do you consider to be the basic fundamental principles of management?

If you get this job what do you consider the strategic actions should be to drive down costs out of the operation?

Give me your definition of quality?

Give me your definition of Total Quality Management?

Make a note of any nasty questions and develop a reply in the event you ever get similar questions.

Appearance

I stood naked in front of the wardrobe mirror and took a good long look at myself. I looked like a pregnant duck, I was overweight and it was all congregated in my stomach. I am five feet seven inches tall; I stood on the scales and weighed 13 stone 7lbs. I thought to myself if a prospective employer looks at me they will think if this guy can't look after himself could I trust him to look after my business. The next day I went to see the nurse in occupational health she gave me a full check over and gave me a clean bill of health with the exception of my weight. I was 2 stone 5lbs overweight. The next weekend I did a trial at the gym and joined up.

Thereafter I put myself through a punishing schedule, I got up at 6:00am every morning and went for a forty-five minute run. Well actually it was more of a brisk walk, I started off jogging then walked then ran again. I went to the gym every day; I started off with a 45 minute routine and gradually built this up to 90 minutes. I lost one stone in weight in the first month and half a stone in the second month. I felt better, looked better and grew in confidence. Although I now have a job I plan to carry on with this routine until I hit my target weight.

I think it very necessary to always look you best at the interview; I would personally always turn up in a suit. Cummins are very much a forward thinking company and in line with modern times operated a dress down policy enabling employees to work in casual clothes. The down side of this is that I had stopped buying business suits so I needed to buy new suits to attend interviews. In my case as I was looking for a senior manager position so I needed to buy three suits. One for the first interview, one for the second in the event I was short listed and a third just in case I had to go back for a third interview in front of a board of directors. This could have been an expensive outlay but it wasn't, I drove 35 miles to visit the Dewhirst Factory shop who supply Marks & Spencer. There I bought three suits for a total of £150, exceptionally good value, you may not have a Dewhirst in your area but you will have other retailers who offer price-discounted clothes.

Checklist on appearance.

It is not my intention to teach my grandmother to suck eggs and most of the items on my checklist will be second nature to most people reading this but it helps sometimes to make sure we have not missed anything.

First impressions count always look smart for the interview, looking good makes you feel good and gives you confidence.

Always wear a business suit for the interview this applies to males and females.

Get you hair cut.

Older males should trim nose and ear hair and maybe consider trimming thick bushy eyebrows.

Make sure there is no grime under your fingernails.

Its ok for females to wear perfume but I would advice males to refrain from wearing after shave to the interview as to strong a smell could overwhelm the interviewer.

Males should avoid turning up to interview wearing ear rings, although we have diversity in the workplace these days there are still a lot of old school managers out there who are prejudice to seeing males wearing earrings.

Polish your shoes.

Have a clean handkerchief.

Selling yourself at the interview.

Your looking good so be confident, smile and if at all possible crack the odd funny remark, it all adds to reducing the tension and relaxing the atmosphere. Ask for a drink it demonstrates confidence and prevents your mouth from drying up with all the talking you are going to be doing.

The advertisement in the newspaper together with the candidate and job profile you got from the recruitment agent provides a basis for developing your interview strategy. This detail gives you background information on the company, the role and the type of person they are looking for. Analyse the detail look for areas that match your strengths, background and experience. From the questions asked look for opportunities to introduce this into your answers.

In the event you do not get an opportunity to raise these issues wait until towards the end of the interview and then take control of the proceedings. You become the interviewer ask leading questions that work there way round to you giving the answer that matches the candidate and experience criteria outlined in the profile. You may find this difficult at first but the more interview experience you get the more proficient you will become. Make sure you have a list of questions you want to ask about the organisation and the role.

When asked a tough or particularly nasty question do not panic, give yourself some breathing space and time to think by replying: That's an excellent question, its taken me by surprise, its one I haven't ever been asked before, I'll just take a couple of seconds to collate my thoughts. This makes the interviewer feel good and gives you some time to think. The more interviews you attend will broaden your horizons to interview styles, techniques and range of questions. Focus on the positive treat every interview as a leaning experience; always get feedback and try to identify your strengths and weaknesses. A good tip is to follow up the interview a few days later by letter thanking them for inviting you to interview, say how much you enjoyed the interview and meeting them and ask for feed back. This demonstrates your continued interest and gives them a memory jogger lifting you to the front of their minds.

Outplacement counselling

It the event things are going badly you are being invited to interview but not getting the jobs then you need to take a step back and consider what is going wrong. Are you seeking feedback following the interview to understand your strengths and weaknesses and what went well and what didn't.

I suspect that if you are getting interviews then what's on your CV must be in line with what the recruitment agent is looking for so you may have a problem with your interview technique.

Are you preparing properly for the interview?

Have you developed you interview strategy based on the requirements of the job?

Do you fully understand what the requirements of the job are?

Are you demonstrating you have the experience, skills and ability to perform the role?

Have you done your research homework on the organisation?

Have you prepared a list of questions to interrogate the interviewer and bring out your ability in relation to the role?

If you feel you are doing all of the above then you may benefit from some professional outplacement counselling. These organisations are well advertised in national and city newspapers. A word of caution though they are expensive so only use them as a last resort. If you are being made redundant from a large company then it is possible that outplacement counselling will be arranged for you as part of your compensation package. The advantage of using an outplacement counselling service is that they will teach you similar techniques to those outlined in this book but will also coach you on interview technique and video you in a mock up interview which you can constantly refer to thereafter to develop you technique and overcome areas of weakness.

Summary

- Prepare forward plans: Self development plan
  Redundancy disaster plan

- Create your CV; prove out its marketing potential by applying for jobs. Get feed back on areas of improvement at interviews.

- Mail shot local agents; follow up with an Email or telephone call.

- Use the Internet: Register with agents.
  Search websites for vacancies.

- Use local and national papers, consider moving up market in addition to your present level. If you don't have a go you will never know.

- Go after the un-advertised jobs market; use business directories to target potential employers.

- Be well prepared for the interview, know the company background, product range and have you list of questions ready. Take control of the interview make sure you bring out your skills, ability and capabilities in relation to the role. At the interview the only information the employer has on you is what you gave him in your CV and covering letter, questions will therefore be based on this detail so anticipate and develop replies.

- Appearance, look good, feel good, be confident, sell yourself and get feed back on your letter of application, CV and the interview.

- If all else fails get help consider outplacement counselling and talking with your local job centre.

- If over 50 and still unemployed after six months register with New Deal 50 Plus.

Overview

I have written this book off the back of my elation at securing a new position so quickly. I wanted to put my thoughts down on paper and provide a useful simple guide to help people in a similar position. The trauma of being made redundant is a gut wrenching experience, it generates incredible amounts of pain and stress and totally destroys one's confidence. When one has a young family, a large mortgage and additional debt you feel a total failure, it is very easy to slip into a life destroying deep depression. I want to stress the importance of planning ahead, sooner or later a very large percentage of the UK population will suffer the indignity of being made redundant. Its not something that happens to other people, sooner of later its going to happen to you, be prepared.

Prepare your forward plan now, prepare your self development plan now and do as I did prepare your strategic redundancy disaster plan. When the black spot falls and the HR department pulls the trigger be wearing your bulletproof vest. Prevent the need to feel sorry for yourself focus on the positive, keep your head up, maintain your confidence and pride in yourself and demonstrate to potential employers there is no substitute for the experience or skills the mature person has to offer.

Remember luck doesn't come into it, be prepared, be positive, be confident, the ball's in your court, make it happen.

Over the hill aged 54? No Sir Absolutely Not!